Isn't Moon Beautiful

Ms. Sania Joy

FIVE ELEMENTS
PUBLISHERS

Copyright

ISBN: 978-81-994569-6-9

Published by Five Elements Publishers

At Five Elements Publishers we strive to enrich the literary world with more diverse authors and progressive ideas so that the world gets a chance to view from unconventional perspective.

We at Five Elements Publishers are committed to encourage original creative content. We assure that we don't provide your creative content to any automated machines. We preserve your original creative content and pass it on to next generations as it is.

Contacts us: online@fiveelementspublishers.com

Visit us: www.fiveelementspublishers.com

*All images are AI generated.

Acknowledgements

I begin with gratitude to God for the strength, patience, and guidance that helped me give shape to these emotions and words.

I am thankful for every experience — love, pain, longing, solitude, and healing — that taught me lessons beyond words. Each moment shaped the thoughts and feelings woven into these pages.

I also extend my heartfelt appreciation to everyone who supported me, believed in me, and stood by me during my quiet struggles.

Finally, I thank my readers for taking this journey with me. May these words offer comfort, understanding, and strength to your heart.

With gratitude,
Ms. Sania Joy

Preface

This book is a small attempt to put feelings into words. It is made of emotions that live quietly in the heart — love, pain, sacrifice, longing, and loneliness. Every poem in this collection reflects moments we all experience but rarely speak about.

These poems talk about the silence of one-sided love, and the heaviness of missing mother's endless love.

They also carry gentle motivation, reminding us that even in pain, there is strength, and even in solitude, there is hope.

The poems are written in simple words, straight from the heart. The images included are chosen to match the emotions of each poem, helping the reader feel the depth of every line.

This book is for those who feel deeply, love truly, and carry emotions quietly. May these pages make you feel understood, comforted, and a little less lonely.

Table of Contents

1. THE MOON AND THE SUN

I am the moon, and you are the sun,
The light that finds me,
The fire that makes me shine.
Your warmth reaches me
Across the endless Moon and Sun.

I am the moon, and you are the sun,
The light that finds me,
The fire that makes me shine.
Your warmth reaches me,
Across the endless sky,
And though we can never touch,
Our love still glows silent, eternal, divine.

Perhaps the world's first love story,
Was written in our light,
For when the universe began,
We were already there,
Two souls, apart yet intertwined.

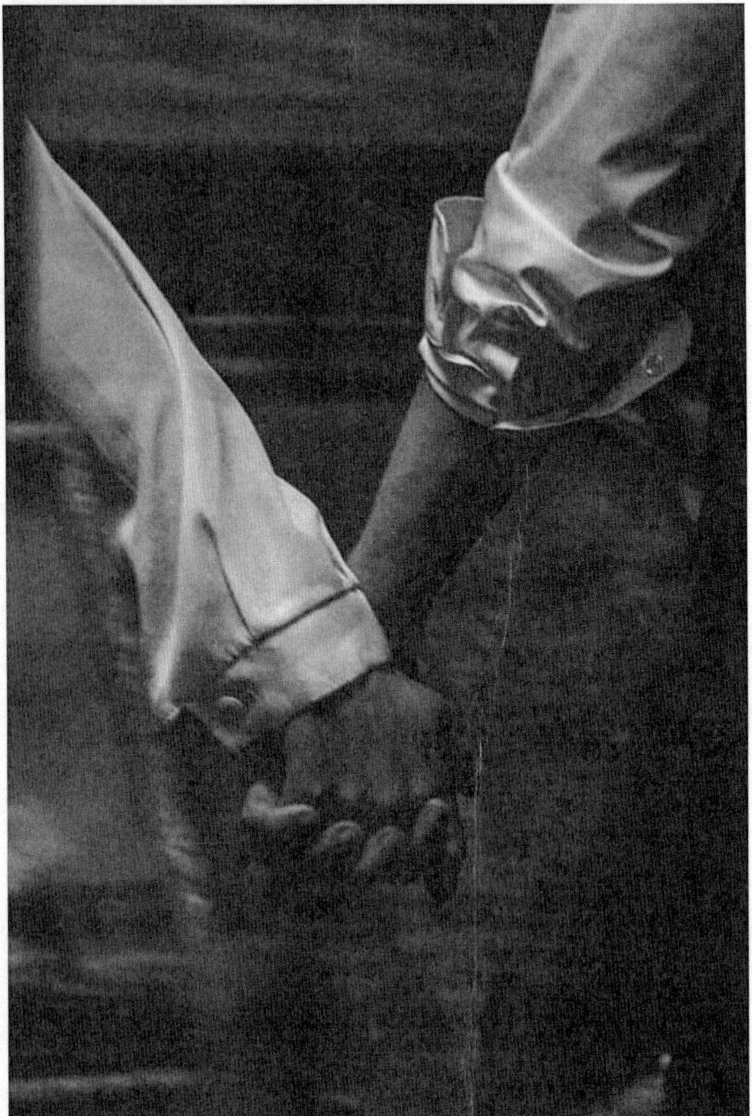

2. UNTOLD DESIRES

There is a new desire in my heart,
Which my heart hesitates to say.
There is a new wish deep inside,
A wish to hold your hands someday.

There lies a long distance between us,
Like the sky and the waiting earth.
Will you shower a rain of love,
And give my soul rebirth?

In the garden of my love,
You are the fluttering butterfly.
Will you sip the honey of my heart,
Before the petals dry?

But my restless crazy heart,
Refuses to understand,
Some desires are meant to stay as desires,
And never reach the hand.

3. SECRET LOVE

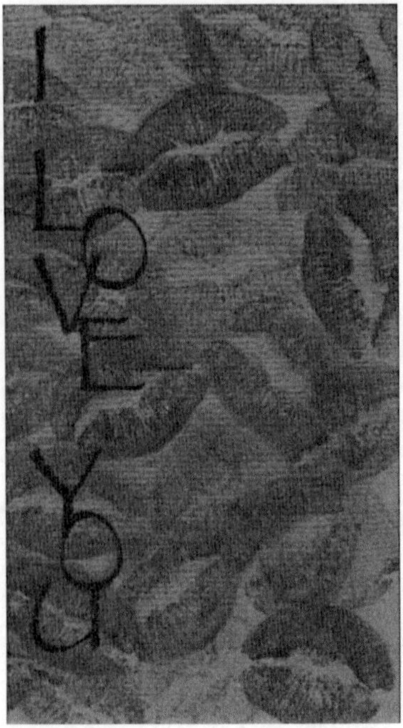

Dear…

You asked me if I love you,

But I had no clear answer.

You asked if we're just friends,

That question created a trouble in my heart,

And still, I couldn't reply.

You asked if we're just friends,

Yet again, I had no answer.

Dear…

My silence doesn't mean

I don't love you.

It means, you are someone beyond an answer.

4. JUST MEMORIES

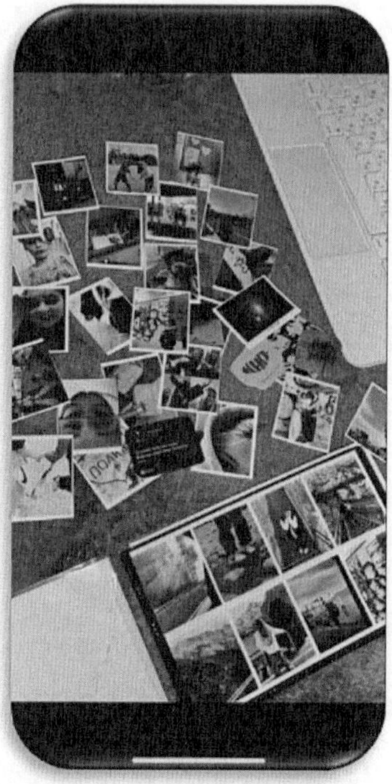

I lost myself in your
thoughts.

My mind buzzes like a
restless bee.

Since the day you left,

This abandoned soul thirsts
for your love.

These nights stretch
endlessly,

My eyes beg to close,

Yet my mind refuses to rest.

Once, under this same moonlight,

We wandered through the streets

With love and laughter

Now, the moonlight feels colder,

For you is just a memory.

5. HUG TO HEART

It started with a hug, slow and smooth,
Like a sweet melody, his lips craved for her.
Why look away, when I am yours,
Oh beloved?
Why be doubtful, when I am yours,
Oh beloved?
Let us forget the time and the world too,
I cannot take my eyes off you, dear.
After seeing you, I wondered if,
God was a sculptor,
For your beauty mesmerized me.
Oh beloved,
Please, lay in my arms for a while,
I'm never enough of being with you.
If anyone asks me what love
The answer is now easy
I'll say your name,
Oh my beloved,
Be with me, now and forever.

6. THE WARMTH OF YOU

This mind was once a cold, lonely glacier,

But your gaze melted it into a gentle sea.

My heart was a rough, unshaped stone,

Until your words smoothed it tenderly.

The warmth you give wraps around me,

Soft and safe — like a mother's womb.

In your presence, I find my peace,

In your love, I find my home.

7. LOVE AT FIRST SIGHT

While walking on a
spring evening,

The time I saw you,

Everything around me,

Felt faded

A new flower of love,

Bloomed in my heart,

With a fragrance of happiness,

An inner voice whispered,

This is the girl for you,

She is the only one for you,

You opened the key to my heart,

And stayed there,

Without my permission.

8. ETERNAL CALM

Slow and soothing like the evening wind,
Your presence wraps my soul within.
In this loud and bustling world of mine,
You are the peace, the sweetest sign.

I know not what virtue I have done,
To earn a heart like yours,
Maybe in prayers of lives long past,
I might whispered your name,
And god heard my prayers.

Now every dawn feels soft and bright,
When your thoughts kiss my morning light.
And if there's life beyond this one's gate,
I wish again — you'll be my mate in my next life too

9. UNPREDICTABLE LOVE

In this fleeting moment,

We stand together,

And that alone is enough for me.

Even if the cruel curse of caste,

Tries to shatter our love,

I'll fight for you,

Till my very last breath.

A life without you,

Is like a fish on land,

Gasping for the water,

That once gave it life,

Your name echoes,

In every breath I take,

It beats softly,

With every throb of my heart.

I don't know,

What destiny will write for us,

Even if fate pulls us,

Onto different roads,

My soul will still wander,

Searching for your love...

Because you are the only one my heart search for

10. LONG DISTANCE

There's a thread between us, Invisible.

Yet strong enough,

To cross the oceans of time and tide.

Each morning,

The first thought that blooms in my mind is you.

You live in my prayers,

You wander through my dreams.

Though miles may lie between our hearts,

I see this distance

As the Lord's way of testing our love.

Let's endure it, my dear

Let's prove we were truly made for each other.

Once, we sat side by side,

Sipping the sweetness of love in each other's eyes.

Now, we connect through thoughts and souls,

For love needs no touch to survive.

The only thing that feels eternal,

The only truth I hold close,

Is my love for you

Just you.

11. IT'S UNFAIR AND UNKNOWN

First I thought it was your fault,

But gradually I accept

And I bow down in this dark cold night

I was the wrong.

My innocent heart like a kid crying for toy...
I begged you to be with

me...

The glass of trust is now shattered and broken
into the pieces which is,

Painted in guilt and gloomy shade.

I'm waiting for the sleep goddess to be kind on
me...

Sleeping tablets started asking excuses for not
doing its work.

My brain asked my heart why only him,

Heart gave a silent answer without uttering a
single word.

It's unfair and unknown, what is happening to me,

The more I try to hate you the more I got hurt,

It's unfair and unknown...

12. ONE-SIDED LOVE

Look at my situation
without you,

Does it seem easy?

Every smile I wear feels
borrowed,

Every heartbeat
whispers your name in
grief.

Don't just see the face I show,

See the beauty of my heart within.

Like air traffic control guides the aircraft,

Your thoughts guide the flight of my soul.

All in the rhythm of your control.

Just one gaze from you is enough,

To turn my storms into peace.

Look at me now, lost without you,

Still, my love for you will never cease.

13. YOU ARE THE

You are the dream that
colours my nights,

The wish that whispers
through my heart,

The rhythm behind
every silent prayer,

The glow that lights my
lonely stars.

You are the heaven my
soul desires,

The joy wrapped in every tear I hide,

The ache that feels like sweetest fire,

The touch that heals and keeps me alive.

You are my faith when hope runs thin,

My tomorrow, my forever within.

Every beat, every breath, every sign —

Leads me back to you, my heart... my divine.

14. THE DAY YOU DEPARTED

The day you
departed,

It felt empty.

I lost the rhythm
of my soul.

Without you,

Where could I go?

I am just a canvas,

You are the paint,

Bringing color to my world,

Turning emptiness into an art.

No one could ever replace you,

For the only one who could…

is you.

15. SOOTHING TO THE HEART

The evening sun's soft light,
Made the sky blush bright,
Soothing to the heart,
Humble and dreamy.
At the horizon's tender line,
The sea kissed the sun,
Soothing to the heart,
Humble and dreamy.

The whispering wind hummed a hymn,
A hymn of love,
Soothing to the heart,
Humble and dreamy.
The waves caressed my feet,
Cool and serene,
Soothing to the heart,
Humble and dreamy.

16. LIKE A DEW ON LEAF

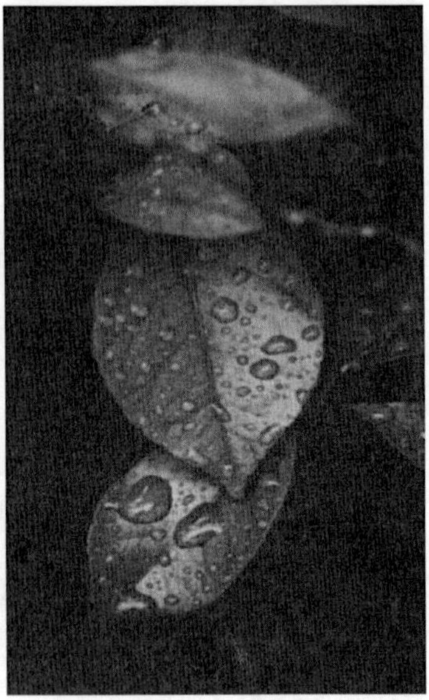

In the silence of the dark night,

Alone in the room looking at myself in the mirror,

With irresistible tears,

Like a dew on leaf,

Pure like pearl,

Slided by my cheeks,

No one to listen,

No one will understand,

The pain my heart bears,

The thoughts my mind bears,

Like heavy cloud waiting for fall,

My feelings are about to burst,

Like a dew on leaf,

Pure like pearl.

17. I'M The SAND

I'm the sand,

You are the sea,

You come to me again
and again.

The wind takes me far,

To places I don't know,

But somehow your
waves always reach me.

I don't know my destination,

I don't know where life will take me,

But the only thing I know is my love for you,

Even if I get lost,

Even if the tides change,

My heart will always wait for you.

Because I'm the sand,

And you are the sea.

18. DELIGHT IN THE MOONLIGHT

Gazing at my watch,

From time to time,

Waiting for her,

With the same hope every minute.

Butterflies rushed in my stomach,

Making me feel excited,

And nervous at the same time.

She stepped into the restaurant,

Wearing a red dress,

Glowing softly under the moonlight.

Her eyes spoke a thousand words,

Before her lips even moved.

My throat trembled,

Struggling to say the first hello.

My mind went blank,

Completely lost in her beauty,

A beauty that felt like magic.

Under the moonlight,

She looked like a dream,

And her eyes...

Said everything.

19. FAVORITE MISTAKE

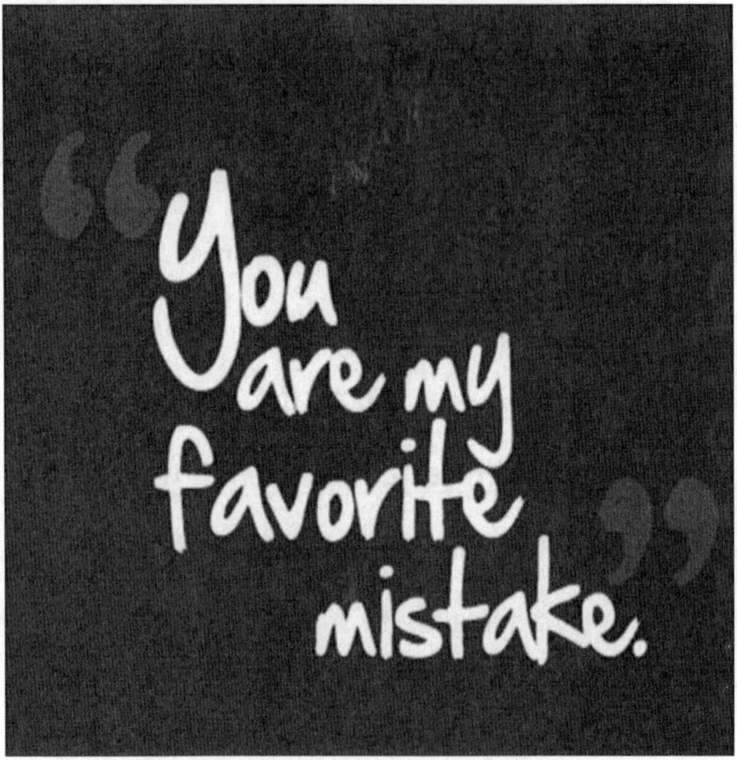

He didn't had mercy on me,

The glass of trust has shattered,

Why can't you break it before!

Now, it's only me and my feelings,

The days we had together,

The songs we sung together,

The walls of our classrooms witnessed our love, still....he didn't had

mercy on me.

The mask of misunderstanding,

Stolen our love,

As a thief in midnight,

Is our love such tremble?,

Last day at this time,

You promised me,

with the moon,

In this new moon,

Moon might felt bad for using its name,

He didn't had mercy on me,

The glass of trust has shattered...

20. NOW YOU ARE HAPPY WITHOUT ME

Now you are happy without me,

And I know that well.

So I'm leaving you,

With a small, unpleasant smile.

I tried to be strong,

But my eyes don’t listen.

They keep looking for you,

In every moment, everywhere.

Tears keep falling,

Not because you left,

But because I still love you.

My eyes want to see you,

Even though it hurts.

They still wait for your love,

A love that is gone now.

I’m walking away today,

Not because I want to,

But because you no longer need me.

21. EVEN THOUGH OUR STORY

Even though our story was incomplete,

It was still pure.

Even though there were struggles,

Ours was the sweetest story of all.

In the darkest days of my life,

You arrived like a gentle ray of dawn,

Touching my heart with the quiet light

Of a love I never knew before.

Now the silence between us stands helpless,

Reflecting the distance our hearts never wanted.

We both see the truth in our situation,

Yet neither of us moves.

Because eyes never lie —

And I can still see love in yours.

So why do we continue this silence?

Why pretend that we don't feel?

Just one call from you is enough

To break every wall between us.

I am here… still waiting…

22. IF YOU ARE MINE

If you are mine,

I won't need anything else in this world.

Let's create a small world of our own,

Where only you and I exist.

Be mine — that's all my heart wants.

Let's start a new life together,

Where our dreams come true, one by one.

I'll stay with you when you laugh,

And stay with you when you cry.

Because the happiness of being with you,

Is something words can never describe.

23. WITHOUT SAYING A SINGLE WORD

She left the world,

Without saying a word,

Without knowing,

She was my whole world.

One day, she asked for a kiss,

I laughed and said no for fun,

Now I wish I had said yes,

Cause that was my last chance with my girl.

I kissed her forehead softly,

My eyes were full of tears,

My heart was full of pain,

And guilt that will never fade.

Yes... she left the world,

Without saying a single word.

24. IN THIS WORLD FULL OF

In this world full of storm,

No storm can turn of fire in my soul,

There is no room in my heart for doubt,

I strongly hold on my values along with me,

Throughout this hard journey.

I will climb the mountain of my dreams,

And will place the flag of success over it,

Like the gold smelted on the fire,

I trust the process,

Diamond was once a coal,

Butterfly was once a pupa,

Beautiful painting was once a canvas,

Tree was once a sapling,

I will climb the mountain of my dreams,

And will place the flag of success over it...

In this world full of storm,

No storm can turn of fire in my soul.

25. WITHOUT EXPECTING ANYTHING IN RETURN

Without expecting anything in return,
She carried you within her womb.
When sickness made your body weak,
She sacrificed her nights for you.

The pain you felt when you fell to the ground
Echoed as deeper pain in her heart.

Without expecting anything in return,
She said she wasn't hungry,
Hiding her hunger behind a smile.

Without expecting anything in return,
She grew tired in the kitchen,
Just to see your stomach filled.

26. WITHOUT BEARING A WOMB

Without bearing a womb,

He protected me in his shield of love,

His words was sweet like lullaby,

Through the heavy rain of crisis,

He unfolded the umbrella of love,

Like a painter's masterpiece,

Amazing and beautiful,

He made my day,

In the path of life,

He walked along,

Like a servant doing service,

Without expecting anything in return,

He served me,

Humble and kind,

Without bearing a womb,

Like a sweet lullaby.

ONE DAY
DAY ONE

27. ONE DAY I WILL

One day, I will rise and touch the sky,

No mountain too high, no storm too strong to stop me.

Let them laugh, let them doubt,

For I carry a fire that only I can see.

I know my journey, I trust my steps,

I believe in the victory waiting for me.

In this life full of dreams and desires,

I will chase every goal with fearless eyes.

And someday, I will look back and smile,

As I strike off every dream I wrote,

From my bucket list,

One by one.